Blues Soloing for Guitar
Volume 1: Blues Basics

Learn and Master
the Basics of Blues Guitar

by James Shipway

Contents

Introduction

Welcome to *Blues Soloing for Guitar*. This is Volume One: *Blues Basics*!

Congratulations on choosing the first book in my *Blues Soloing for Guitar* series. You're about to learn much of what you need to know to sound like a great blues guitarist.

So many books, lessons and videos make becoming a good blues guitarist seem like a daunting prospect. They make it sound as if there is *so much* to learn, you wonder how you'll ever understand it all!

Well, I want to let you in on a little secret...

You *don't* need to know much at all to play great blues guitar. Most of the greatest blues music uses the same simple chord sequence and a few basic scales. It's how blues musicians *use* these materials that make for great music.

The problem is, many books and lessons give you the *materials* blues musicians use, but don't really teach you *how* to use them. They give you a few scales, a few licks, then they leave the rest up to you!

That's where my **Blues Soloing for Guitar** books are different: I've attempted to give you most of the blues knowledge you'll probably ever need as well as authentic blues examples showing you *how* to use this knowledge.

Volume 1 is all about building the rock-solid foundation you need to become a great blues player.

We'll be looking at the tools blues musicians use to make music, things like the blues scale, the minor pentatonic scale, sliding scales and the 12 bar blues.

We'll study essential blues techniques like string bending, blues curls and vibrato and I'll be making sure that you know how to do them the *right* way.

I'll also show you how you can take all of this and begin playing blues licks and solos that sound like the greatest blues players the world has ever seen!

After that you'll be all set to carry on our lessons together in **Blues Soloing for Guitar, Volume 2**. There we'll look at some more advanced blues tools and concepts.

I'm not saying that you'll become a killer blues player overnight, but I promise that if you work through these lessons thoroughly, following my instructions, you'll begin to develop the skills and knowledge that today's blues player needs. You'll also be well on your way to developing an all-important 'blues vocabulary' so that eventually you'll be *so* familiar with the blues language, that you'll just instinctively know what to play to make your solos sound great!

How Should You Use This Book?

Just going through these lessons probably won't turn you into a good blues guitarist; there's more to it than that. Let's quickly look at what you'll need to do to get awesome results with this book.

1. Don't Skip Chapter 1: 'The Basics You Need To Play Awesome Blues'

This is the most important chapter in this book and without the knowledge it gives you, playing blues is going to be an uphill struggle. Even if some of what's covered seems too basic for you, read through it anyway just to make sure you know it all. I cover the basics in this book because *not* understanding them is what holds *most* players up!

2. Lesson Order

If you're reading this book then I'm guessing you're either a beginner or intermediate blues guitarist and I'd suggest going through the lessons in order. This is because the knowledge and concepts I give you in each lesson follow on from what you learned in the previous ones.

If you're a more experienced blues guitarist using this book for some fresh ideas and perspective, you may want to pick your own route through the lessons. Be aware that I will refer back to topics covered in earlier chapters, so if you need something explained you may need to backtrack a little.

3. Watch the Mini Lessons / Demonstrations and Get the Backing Tracks!

To help you hear how each solo is supposed to sound I've set up a website to accompany this book series. There you can see me playing each solo over a backing track and watch lessons and demonstrations on some of the important tools and techniques covered in this book.

You can also grab the audio recording of me performing each solo as well as downloading the backing tracks to practice over.

There's *lots* of cool stuff there to really supplement everything in this book so make sure to check it out at **www.bluesguitarbook.com**

4. Take It Steady...

If you're anything like me, then the temptation to rush through a new book can be overwhelming! It's almost as though we think that working through the lessons faster will help us learn to do everything sooner. I'm here to tell you from experience that the opposite is true!

Take your time working through each lesson. Rushing won't get you the end result you bought this book for.

5. Study the *Blues Power Moves* (Important!)

Rather than only ever copying other players, you should aim to be able to write and improvise your *own* solos. To do this you'll need a *vocabulary* of soloing ideas which you can play and use.

The Blues Power Moves section at the end of each lesson will help you build this vocabulary by teaching you the most versatile and useful ideas used in the solo. Take each Blues Power Move and experiment with it. Over time it will become a part of your soloing vocabulary and you'll find yourself using it without even knowing you're doing so!

Experimentation is the key here. I suggest following this approach with each Power Move:

- Learn the **Blues Power Move**
- Notice where it fits into whichever scale shape it comes from (so you can find it and use it)
- Make up two licks (or more!) of your own which use the Power Move. Tab them out in your *'Guitar Practice Workbook'* *
- Practice using it over a backing track. Experiment with it, play around with it, add bits to it etc
- See if you can create some exercises of your own to get you playing with these ideas

Don't underestimate the importance of these Blues Power Moves. Follow these suggestions and over time you'll see your soloing vocabulary and your blues guitar skills grow and grow.

You're all set...

That's about it for now, time to jump into the first lesson. Good luck and I hope you enjoy the journey of discovery you're about to embark on.

I'll see you in **Lesson 1**...

* *The Guitar Practice Workbook* (by me, James Shipway) is a blank tab and fretboard diagram book which also contains practice hacks, scales and chord shapes. I use this book daily myself during my practice sessions to record licks, exercises and song ideas. You can find it on **Amazon**.

Lesson 1:
The Basics You Need
To Play Awesome Blues Guitar

You probably can't wait to grab your guitar and rip straight into the solos in this book... and that's great!

But wait!

Before you begin, we need to make sure you have an understanding of the following basic tools used to play blues guitar:

- **12 Bar Blues**
- **The Minor Pentatonic Scale**
- **The Blues Scale**

These tools are what the *greatest* blues guitarists use 95% of the time. I'm talking about blues legends like **Eric Clapton, BB King, Albert King** and **Stevie Ray Vaughan**!

Obviously, learning to make these tools sound like those players is the real challenge, but first we need to equip you with what you need to know. Let's do that now...

The 12 Bar Blues

Most blues songs are based on the ***12 bar blues***. This is the framework or 'blank canvas' blues musicians use to make music. If you were playing a song with a blues band, you'd most likely be playing a 12 bar blues.

So, what is the 12 bar blues?

It's simply a chord sequence which is **12 bars long** and consists of **3** chords. These chords are normally played as ***dominant 7th*** chords (chords with names like A7, D7, E7).

The following image shows the most common way to play the 12 bar blues. It's shown in the key of A (more on keys later). I've given you some possible chord shapes to use, but you can use different ones if you prefer.

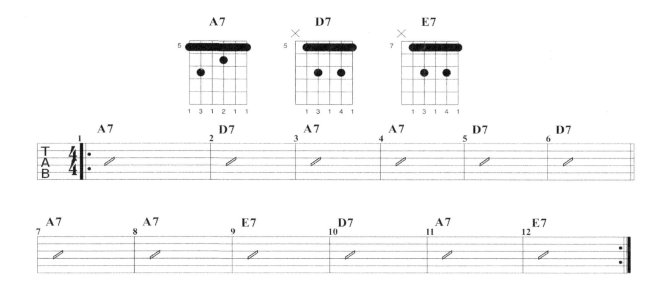

Notice it's 12 bars long and uses three dominant 7th chords: A7, D7 and E7. If you took any chord shapes you knew for A7, D7 and E7 and played through the chord sequence, then you would be playing a 12 bar blues in the key of A.

Do the chords always have to be in the same order?

Yes. The 12 bar blues has a fixed order for the chords and you can't just put them in any order you choose. The order of the chords is part of what makes it the 12 bar blues.

Having said that, there are simple variations which you'll see in this book. Don't worry about this for now, just get familiar with the most common form of the 12 bar blues like I've given you here.

How is the 12 bar blues used by blues musicians?

In performance, the 12 bar blues is repeated multiple times. There might be singing, a guitar solo, a harmonica solo or anything else taking place over the top of it... but the basic 12 bar blues framework will normally remain the same throughout.

This is how blues musicians can 'jam' or play together without any preparation whatsoever. As long as they know the 12 bar blues, they have a common framework they can use to make music together.

So, in summary...

Think of the 12 bar blues as the most common 'song' you'll use when you play blues.

There's a little bit more you need to know and we'll be returning to the 12 bar blues later to build on this basic knowledge.

Note: See the chord shape reference section at the back of this book (Appendix 2) for some chord shapes you could use to play the 12 bar blues.

The Minor Pentatonic Scale

Simply think of a scale as a set of notes with a certain sound and think of a **pentatonic** scale as a scale containing just **5** notes.

For playing blues the most common scale is the **minor pentatonic scale**. When you hear a blues guitarist soloing, there's a very good chance he's using this scale. Think of it as a collection of notes which just work well with the 12 bar blues chord sequence.

The most convenient way to learn the minor pentatonic scale on the guitar is using a scale pattern. Let's look at the most commonly used pattern. This pattern is often called '**shape 1 minor pentatonic**' and this is how I will refer to it in this book. It contains 5 notes and each one is just played more than once. Here it is in the key of A:

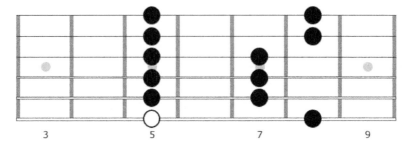

The minor pentatonic scale is the default scale for playing licks and solos in blues music, it's essential that you know it! If necessary, stop now and take 5-10 minutes to memorise the scale pattern.

Using the 12 Bar Blues and the Minor Pentatonic Scale Together

So how do the 12 bar blues and the minor pentatonic scale fit together?

Simple: the notes in the scale are used over the 12 bar blues to create melodies, licks, and solos.

So, if you were jamming with a guitar player and he or she was playing a 12 bar blues, you could solo over the top using *only* the minor pentatonic scale shape.

The scale is like your 'ingredients' for cooking up great blues solos and believe it or not, you can play amazing blues solos even if the minor pentatonic is the *only* scale you know how to play. This is because the minor pentatonic scale will work over the **entire 12 bar blues chord sequence**.

Let me repeat that last bit: it's important!

There is *no need* to use any other scale at all, even when the chords change in the 12 bar blues. The minor pentatonic scale works all over it. Most of the *greatest* blues solos ever use this simple approach.

That's not to say that blues guitarists never use *other* approaches as well, but this 'one scale' approach is the most common and it's definitely the best place to start.

You *do* need to be in the correct key though! Let's look at that next...

Changing the Key of the Scale

It's important to use the scale in the same key as the 12 bar blues you want to play over.

For example, in the key of A you need to use the A minor pentatonic scale. For a 12 bar blues in the key of G, use the G minor pentatonic scale and so on.

The shape 1 minor pentatonic scale shape can easily be put into any key, you just move it to a different place on the neck.

It works like this...

The scale pattern has what is called a 'root note'. This note is used to determine *where* to play the scale for any key. Below is shape 1 minor pentatonic again. The root note is on the low E string shown as a hollow white dot:

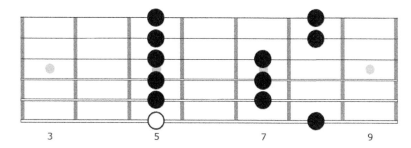

Here are the notes F, G, A, B, C, D and E along the low E string:

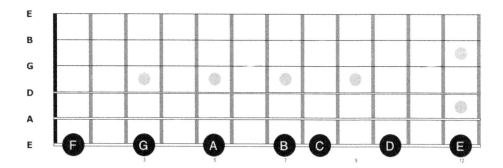

To move the scale into a particular key, simply line up the root note in the scale pattern with the note for the key you need.

For example, if you need a G minor pentatonic scale:

1. Find G on the low E string. Look on the diagram and you'll see it's at the **3rd** fret
2. Now, simply take the same scale pattern but play it with the root note on the E string at the **3rd** fret

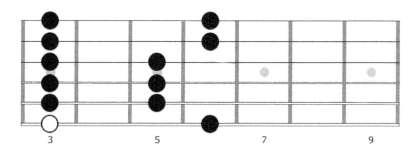

You just played a G minor pentatonic scale which you could use to jam over a 12 bar blues in G.

If you needed to play a B minor pentatonic scale:

1. Find B on the low E string, it's at the **7th** fret
2. Begin the scale pattern with the root note at the **7th** fret and the result is B minor pentatonic.

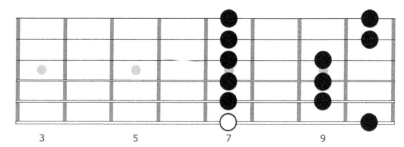

So, once you know the notes along the low E string you can easily move this scale pattern around and jam in any key, an essential skill for any blues musician!

The fretboard diagram below shows you the notes along the low E string. I've included the sharp and flat notes this time:

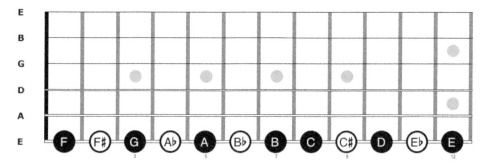

Using the scale pattern, how would you play the following minor pentatonic scales?

- **F** minor pentatonic
- **C** minor pentatonic
- **A** minor pentatonic
- **G** minor pentatonic
- **E** minor pentatonic
- **D** minor pentatonic
- **B*b*** minor pentatonic
- **F#** minor pentatonic
- **E*b*** minor pentatonic

Answers: Play the scale starting at these frets for each key: **F**:1st fret, **C**:8th fret, **A**:5th fret, **G**:3rd fret, **E**:12th fret, **D**:10th fret, **B*b***:6th fret, **F#**:2nd fret, **E*b***:11th fret.

The Blues Scale

By adding one extra note to the minor pentatonic we can get the *blues scale*. This gives us a 6 note scale with a darker, more bluesy sound.

Simply take the shape 1 minor pentatonic pattern and add the extra note (shown as black diamond shapes) on the A and G strings. The result is the ***shape 1 blues scale***:

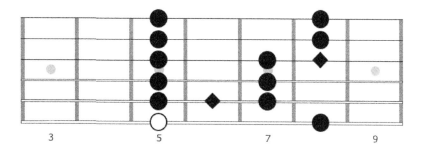

Play the two scales side by side and hear the difference. The added note is the 'flattened 5th interval' and creates a more dramatic, dissonant sound. To learn more about 'flattened 5ths' and *intervals* see chapters 5 and 6 of my '***No Bull Music Theory for Guitarists***' book.

The blues scale can be moved into different keys too: simply use the root note on the low E string as you did before.

So, now you've got two scales: which one should you use when playing blues?

The answer? Both of them!

The two scales are so similar that blues musicians tend to think of them as the same thing and use them *interchangeably*.

Don't let this confuse you! Get used to using the minor pentatonic, but at the same time know you can add in the extra note when you want to for a more bluesy flavour. When you do that, you are technically playing the blues scale.

That's all you need to know to get started!

Of course, you could learn more about chords and scales than what I've taught you in this chapter, but for now you don't really need to. Blues is, by definition, a fairly simple style of music and you'll be amazed at how much great blues guitar can be played with just these simple tools and concepts.

Throughout this book I'll be introducing some more scales and ideas when necessary. For now though, you're ready for the first solo. After studying everything in this chapter it'll make a lot more sense!

Before you move on, test yourself with the questions that follow. Then check your answers against those I've given you. Go back through this chapter and double check anything you got wrong or don't understand.

In the next lesson you'll learn about one of the most crucial blues guitar techniques you'll need to know: string bending. You'll also learn how to play *Kickin' Off*: a cool 12 bar blues guitar solo. See you then!

Now, Test Yourself on Blues Guitar Basics!

1. Most blues songs are based on the _____. This chord sequence is _____ long and consists of three chords. These chords are normally played as _____ chords.

2. What is the pentatonic scale you will use the most when you play blues?

3. When the chords change in the 12 bar blues, you need to change the scale you are playing. True or false?

4. If you were soloing over a 12 bar blues in the key of A you could use the _____ scale over the whole chord sequence.

5. If you were soloing over a 12 bar blues in the key of E you could use the _____ scale over the whole chord sequence.

6. The blues scale is like the minor pentatonic with an added note. The proper name for this added note is the _____.

7. True or false? The blues scale and minor pentatonic scales tend to be used interchangeably.

Check Your Answers and Let's See How You Did:

1. Most blues songs are based on the *12 bar blues*. This chord sequence is *12 bars long* and consists of three chords. These chords are normally played as *dominant 7th* chords.

2. The most common pentatonic scale we use in blues is the *minor pentatonic scale*.

3. *False!* When the chords change in the 12 bar blues, you *don't* need to change the scale you are playing. The minor pentatonic scale played in the key you are in will work over the *entire* 12 bar blues chord sequence!

4. If you were soloing over a 12 bar blues in the key of A you could use the *A minor pentatonic scale* over the whole chord sequence.

5. If you were jamming over a 12 bar blues in the key of E you could use the *E minor pentatonic scale* over the whole chord sequence.

6. The blues scale is like the minor pentatonic with an added note. The proper name for this added note is the *flattened 5th* (this can also be written as *b5*).

7. *True!* The blues scale and minor pentatonic scales tend to be used *interchangeably.*

Further Reading

I've tried to give you an overview of chord and scale theory here as it relates to playing blues. See my '*No Bull Music Theory for Guitarists*' book for no-nonsense lessons about pentatonic and blues scales, intervals, chords and chord sequences. You'll find it on **Amazon**.

Use the tab below to write out any ideas you discover whilst working through this chapter.

Lesson 2:
String Bending, Blues Curls
and *Kickin' Off* Solo Study

If you haven't played any blues solos before, then **Kickin' Off** is a great place to start, teaching you essential techniques and how to pull cool sounding blues ideas out of the minor pentatonic/blues scales from the last chapter.

Kickin' Off will help you start to form a blues soloing vocabulary and even if you have some knowledge of blues already, you'll probably still find some hidden gems in this solo which you can take and use. Before we jump in, let's look at a crucial blues guitar technique being used in this solo: **string bending**.

String Bending: The Sound of Blues Guitar

As with any technique, it's helpful if you can *watch* it being done. That's why this book also comes with online video lessons! Make sure to check out my video on string bending to see everything in this lesson up close at **www.bluesguitarbook.com**

String bending is the technique of 'pushing' the guitar strings with our fingers to play different notes. Bending gives us some of the most expressive and unique sounds available on the guitar and nowhere is this truer than when playing blues. Without string bending, it just doesn't sound like blues!

The two most common string bends are the tone or full-step bend (bending the note up so that it sounds like the note two frets higher) and the semi-tone or half-step bend (bending the note to sound like the note one fret higher). These are notated as 'full' and '½' in guitar tab (see image).

You *can* bend *more* than a tone however and we'll be seeing some bigger bends in some of the solos in this book series.

The importance of mastering bending cannot be over stressed; nothing spoils the sound of someone's playing like the sound of sloppy, out of tune bends!

Bending Hand Position

Having the correct hand position can make the difference between awesome sounding bends and bends which fall short of the mark. Below are the main considerations when it comes to a good bending hand position. Watch the accompanying mini lesson and demonstration at **www.bluesguitarbook.com**

Thumb Over The Top!

Some players will tell you that your thumb should be *behind* the neck and sometimes this is true, but when it comes to bending, that's a bad idea.

Keep your thumb solidly over the top of the neck when you bend, don't let it slip down behind the neck. This gives you the grip, control and stability you need to master bending and get your bends sounding awesome!

'Back Up' Your Bending Finger With Previous Fingers

Wherever possible, use more than one finger to execute the bend. For example, when bending with your third finger, your first and second fingers should also be helping to push the string.

This gives you the pushing power you need to bend strings accurately. It also helps you keep your grip on the string as you bend, so back up those bends whenever possible.

'Pin' the String As You Bend

It should feel as if you are 'pinning' the string to the fretboard as you bend it. If you don't, you could lose your grip on the string or the note will die out too soon.

How To Bend

Once you've got the hand position nailed, how do you actually execute the bend? This is the part that many people get wrong (including me when I started out!) so let's make sure you get off on the right track.

Rotate the Wrist

Many players try to bend by simply 'pushing the string up' with their fingers but this is definitely *not* the best method. Instead, *rotate the wrist* to move the string. This gives you all the strength of your wrist and hand to move the string with, meaning better control and much better sounding bends.

Upwards or Downwards?

When bending we can either push the string upwards or pull it downwards towards the floor. Which should you use?

As a general rule, bend the G, B and top E strings upwards. These are the most common strings to bend, so you'll be bending upwards most of the time. When bending notes on the D, A and low E strings it is normally best to pull the string downwards.

Remember that whether you're bending a string up or pulling it down, the same technique guidelines apply, so keep backing up, have your thumb over the top of the neck and all that good stuff!

So that's your bending crash course...

If you're new to bending this might seem like a lot to take in. That's ok, the important thing is to get into the habit of bending correctly. Don't worry if it takes a while to feel natural, just keep checking you're not straying from the technique guidelines mentioned above. If you've been bending strings already, check you're doing everything right, then your bending technique won't let you down when you need it.

Making It Sound Bluesy: The 'Blues Curl'

See me demo the blues curl up close at **www.bluesguitarbook.com**

There is an important type of bend we hear the great blues players use called a 'blues curl'. This is normally notated in tab as a 'quarter' bend (¼) as shown in this image. Adding a blues curl to a note gives it a beautiful, bluesy character and learning to use them adds a powerful boost to your blues soloing skills!

Think of a blues curl as a small bend added to the *very end* of a note. Of course, learning to use blues curls will take a little practice and it's easier when you know what they sound like. Listen carefully to what blues curls sound like when I play them and try to get yours sounding similar, then you'll begin to get the hang of using this powerful and expressive blues soloing tool.

The *Kickin' Off* solo up next gives you the perfect opportunity to practice and develop your bending in a musical setting. Let's get into that now.

Blues Solo 1: *Kickin' Off*

Description:	A slow blues solo full of essential blues techniques, licks and phrases!
Key:	A
Will improve your:	String bending technique, knowledge of the blues scale, fret hand stretch
Watch me play it here:	**www.bluesguitarbook.com**

The next image gives you a lick-by-lick breakdown of the *Kickin' Off* solo to help you learn it. Follow the performance notes and tips I give you as they'll make sure you're developing good playing habits and will help you get the solo sounding great!

You might just want to focus on being able to play a 'rough' version of the solo before you worry about adding in small details like blues curls. These are the 'polish' you can add once you know the licks and can play them in time. Let's take a look at the full solo:

Scales Used in *Kickin' Off*

All the licks in this solo come from shape 1 A blues scale:

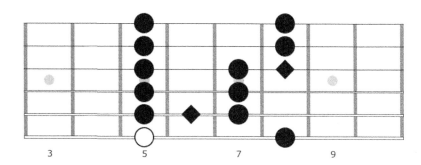

Remember, if you leave out the added note (shown by a black diamond) you get A minor pentatonic!

Lick 1

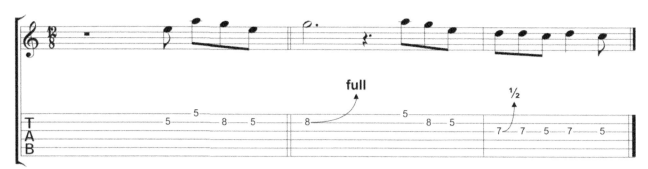

This lick shows you a classic way to begin a blues solo.

- Learn and remember this opening lick, knowing a few strong ways to begin your solos is a good idea!
- I'd suggest using your 1st and 3rd fingers to play most of this lick
- Persevere with the 3 fret stretch between your 1st and 3rd fingers, even if it feels tricky at first. Being able to comfortably do this stretch is very handy
- The lick uses two common blues bends: the full-step bend on the B string and the half-step bend on the G string. Make sure you are using the correct bending techniques when you execute these bends!
- After you've bent the string up, gently touch it with the fleshy part of your picking hand to 'choke off' the bend. This stops us hearing the sound of the bend being let back down again. Sometimes we want to hear the bends being let down, but not in this lick

Lick 2

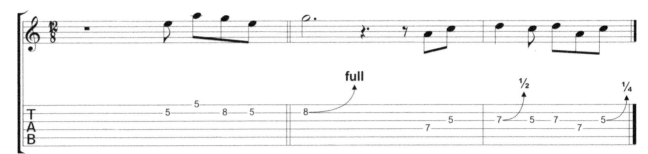

Repetition is an important part of the blues. It gives a solo structure and helps it make musical sense. This lick is a great example of using repetition, it's basically Lick 1 with a different ending!

- Make sure you're bending correctly!
- We're adding a blues curl to the last note in this lick. Remember, it must be added to the end of the note because if you add it straight away it will probably just sound out of tune

Lick 3

A good bending exercise this lick!

- 'Choke off' each bend before letting it down. This will really tidy up your bending
- One more time… check you're bending correctly (thumb over top, backing up, rotating your wrist etc)

Lick 4

Nothing too tricky here...

- Make sure the half-step bend is in time and in tune
- Practice getting the blues curl in the third bar sounding right

Lick 5

A bend we haven't seen yet is being used in this lick. It's on the top E string and is another common blues bending move.

- The top E bend in the second bar takes a bit of strength! Be sure to back up and use your wrist to move the string. Be patient with this bend, if you're new to string bending it's going to take a bit of practice to master

Lick 6

The solo finishes with this simple ending lick. It's really just descending the blues scale pattern but wraps everything up nicely

- Nothing too tricky here. Just get the timing and the rhythm of the phrase solid

That's about it!

If you're new to playing blues then there will be a few things here to get used to. Whatever you do, persevere: this solo lays the foundation for much of what is coming in the rest of the solos in this book.

Don't forget to check out the mini lesson and video demo of *Kickin' Off* at **www.bluesguitarbook.com**

While you're there, download the audio demo and free backing track that goes with the solo. You'll want to practice the solo along to these at some point.

Kickin' Off: Blues Power Moves

Below are some of the key components making up the licks in *Kickin' Off*. These will help you to start building your blues soloing vocabulary.

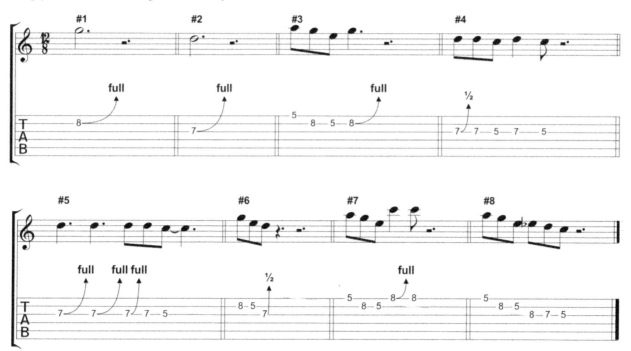

Remember:

- Learn each **Blues Power Move**
- Practice finding each one in the shape 1 blues and minor pentatonic scale shapes they come from
- Make up two licks of your own based on each move. Tab them out in your '**Guitar Practice Workbook**' *
- Practice using these ideas over the *Kickin' Off* backing track. Use them to compose your own solo in the style of *Kickin' Off*, or to practice improvising licks or solos of your own

Good luck with everything in this lesson. When you're ready I'll see you in the next lesson where we'll be looking at the *vibrato* technique and learning a wicked rock-blues solo in the style of Billy Gibbons of ZZ Top!

* **The Guitar Practice Workbook** by James Shipway (2019), find it on **Amazon**.

Use the tab below to write out any ideas you discover whilst working through this chapter.

Lesson 3:
Vibrato Technique and
Sweet William Solo Study

Welcome back!

In this lesson you'll learn **Sweet William**, a blues-rock solo based on the playing of guitarists like Gary Moore and Billy Gibbons (ZZ Top). This will help you to solidify the concepts and techniques from Lesson 1. We'll also be examining another important blues technique: **vibrato**. Let's get started!

Vibrato Technique

See me demonstrate vibrato and show you the technique up close in the accompanying online video lesson at: **www.bluesguitarbook.com**

Vibrato is when we make a note 'shake' or 'wobble' in pitch to give it more expression, like a singer might do with their voice.

In guitar tablature a 'wiggly line' over the top of a note tells you to add vibrato to it. In the following example, vibrato is being added to the third note.

All the great blues guitarists use vibrato. In some cases, it is one of the most recognisable characteristics of their guitar style. Listen to BB King or Freddie King to hear a fast, 'shallow' vibrato or Stevie Ray Vaughan or Gary Moore to hear a 'wider', more aggressive vibrato style.

Just as with string bending there are certain guidelines to follow if you want to develop good vibrato technique.

Hand Position For Vibrato

A good bending hand position will also work well for vibrato, giving you the strength and control to get a rich, warm vibrato happening in your playing.

So, remember the hand position from the previous lesson:

- Thumb over the top of the neck
- Unless you're using your 1st finger, 'back up'
- 'Pin' the string to the fingerboard to stop the note from dying out

If necessary, refer back to the section on string bending in the previous lesson for clarification on any of these points and watch the video lesson to see the hand position in use.

How To Vibrato

So how do you add vibrato to a note? Just as with bending, pin the string firmly with your finger and rotate your wrist to move it. Then move your wrist back again to where it started, causing the note to return back to it's starting position. Doing this repeatedly causes you to bend and release the note multiple times. The resulting changes in pitch create the sound of vibrato.

Grab any note on the guitar and try it. Can you hear a change in the pitch of the note each time? Persevere for a moment if you don't hear it.

'Push' and 'Pull' Vibrato

As with string bending, strings can be moved in an upward or downward motion to get vibrato.

'Push' vibrato is when you push the string upwards and 'pull' vibrato (yep, you guessed it …) is when you pull the string downwards. Which method you should use depends on which string you are playing. In general, use 'push' vibrato on the top E and B strings and 'pull' vibrato on the D, A and low E strings.

On the G string I use push *or* pull vibrato, depending on which finger I'm using and what feels right at the time! Experiment with both methods on this string to get an idea of what works best for you.

How much should you aim to move the string as you vibrato?

Some players favour a 'wide' vibrato, where the pitch changes a lot, giving the vibrato a more aggressive sound. Other players tend to use a 'shallower' vibrato, where the pitch change is less.

I think it's a good idea to practice them both. The strength and control you develop will give you the flexibility to do whatever is going to work best in the moment.

Listen to some of your favourite blues players and notice how they vibrato. What kind of sound do they get? Perhaps you can you get your vibrato sounding the same?

3 Vibrato Mistakes To Avoid!

There are some common vibrato mistakes that I see time and time again. Avoid them and your journey towards great vibrato will be much smoother!

Mistake 1: No Rhythmic 'Pulse'!

Good vibrato tends to be rhythmic. In other words, you don't hear an out of control 'wobble', but instead you hear a rhythmic 'pulsing'. This is going to mean slowing it down and getting the rhythm *under control* as you vibrato.

Mistake 2: Random Pitch Changes!

With each 'cycle' of vibrato (bend and release movement) aim for a similar change in pitch so the vibrato sounds smooth, even and controlled.

So, listen to your vibrato and ask yourself: are the changes in pitch regular, or are they random and out of control?

Mistake 3: Vibrato Sounds Out of Tune!

When you release the bend, make sure the note goes all the way back down to where it started. Sometimes people hold it 'in between' the starting note and the bent note because it feels easier this way. Trouble is, their vibrato sounds like an out of tune bend (not good!). So, remember, let the string all the way back to it's starting point when you release it.

So That's Your Crash Course on Vibrato...

Just as with string bending, it takes a while before the vibrato technique feels natural and easy. Check you're not straying from the technique guidelines I've given you and be patient: nobody gets great vibrato overnight!

I've deliberately put some long notes with vibrato into the *Sweet William* solo to give you the chance to practice this crucial technique.

Let's get into the solo now.

Blues Solo 2: *Sweet William*

Description:	A slow rock blues in the style of guitarists like Billy Gibbons and Gary Moore
Key:	E
Will improve your:	Soloing in the key of E, string bending and vibrato technique, knowledge of the blues scale
Watch me play it here:	**www.bluesguitarbook.com**

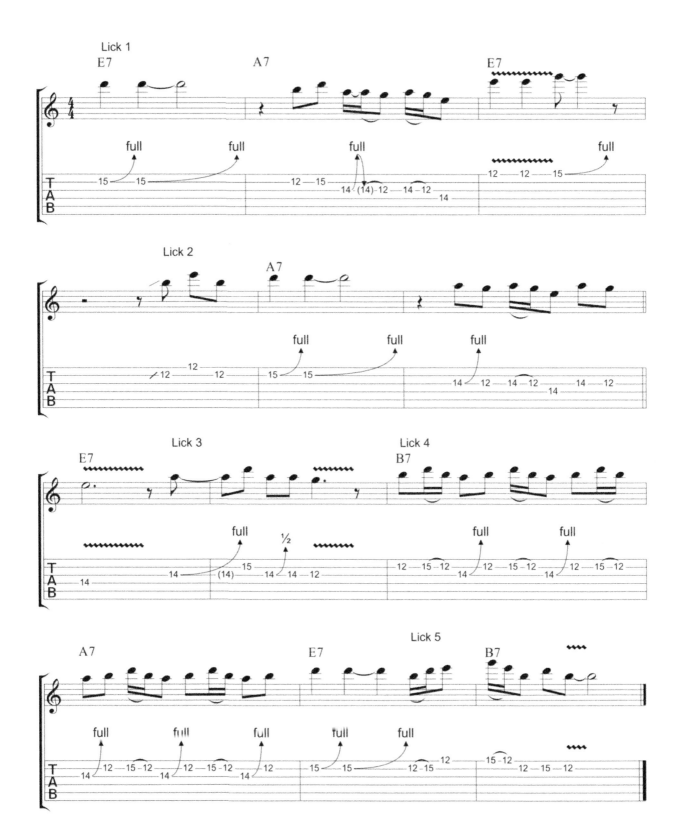

Below you'll find the breakdown of *Sweet William*. Follow the performance notes and tips as you go, they'll help you get it sounding great!

Scales Used in *Sweet William*

This solo is in the key of E so we've moved our minor pentatonic scale pattern up to the 12th fret. Refer back to Lesson 1 if this seems confusing!

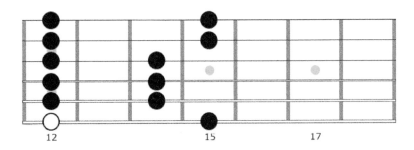

Lick 1

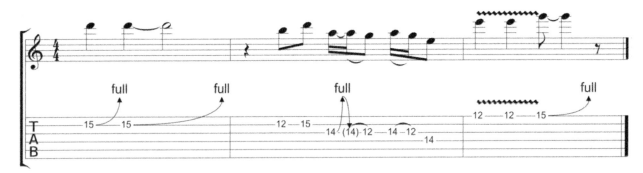

The first lick in the solo uses long, sustaining bends and some common pentatonic pull-off ideas. These will help you become more fluent at using this crucial scale.

- Check your bending technique and tuning as you execute the 15th fret bend on the B string. I suggest using your 3rd finger (backed up with your 1st and 2nd fingers) for the bend. Keep 'pinning' the string to the fingerboard as you hold the bend up; this will make it sing out and sustain (instead of fading out)
- In bar 2 we move further down into the minor pentatonic scale shape for some licks using a combination of bends and pull-offs. Use your 3rd finger for the bends and keep your 1st finger down at the 12th fret, this way it is in position and ready for the pull-offs and you'll get this section flowing and smooth
- The final part of this lick moves up onto the top E string. Use your 1st finger to add 'push vibrato' to the held note at the 12th fret. Then use your 3rd finger, backed up with your 1st and 2nd fingers for the final bend. This bend may take a bit of 'push' to get in tune, so put that bending technique to work!

Lick 2

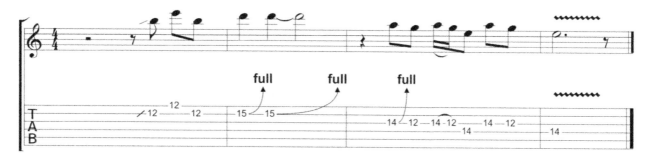

This is a similar idea to Lick 1. The use of repetition helps give the solo a sense of structure, making the licks sound as though they belong together.

- The lick begins by playing the B and top E strings at the 12th fret. Use your 1st finger for both of these notes. To stop them ringing together, 'roll' the pressure across the strings with your finger. This will fret the note you do want and release the pressure from the note you don't want to hear. This technique is important for developing clarity in your licks, so persevere with it, even if it feels strange at first

- The bends and pull-offs in the third bar should be played in the same way as in Lick 1. You'll need to employ the 'rolling' technique here too. Use a 3rd finger roll to play the 14th fret on the D string and the next note on the G string at the 14th fret. This isn't the only way to play this, but it'll get you used to this handy technique

- Use your 3rd finger (backed up with your 1st and 2nd fingers) to add 'pull-vibrato' to the final note in this lick. Follow all the vibrato guidelines given earlier in this chapter!

Lick 3

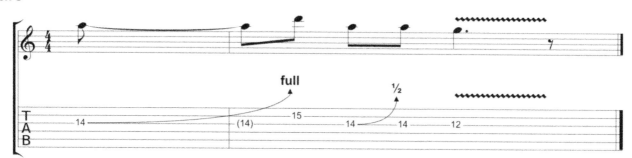

A cool bending lick and a great bending exercise rolled into one!

- Use your 3rd finger (backed up of course!) to bend the 14th fret on the G string. Keeping the bend held up, use your 4th finger to play the 15th fret on the B string. Then 'choke off' the bend and let it down before bending it up again a half-step and continuing through the rest of this phrase. This may all feel a little awkward to start with but it's a common bending lick you need to be able to master

● Needless to say, check you're bending correctly (thumb over top, backing up, rotating your wrist etc) as you play this lick

● 'Pull vibrato' is added to the final note in this lick. Use your 1st finger for this

Lick 4

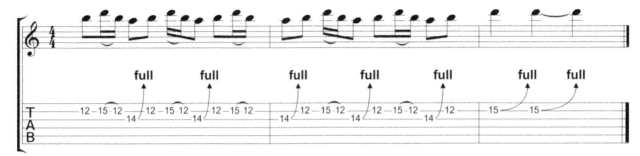

This is an example of a 'repeating lick'. Looping a short phrase around and around creates tension and movement in a solo. It's a simple but effective trick heard in the playing of guitarists like Gary Moore, Jimi Hendrix, Eric Clapton and others. It's important to break longer licks like this up into smaller fragments. Once you've mastered playing the basic repeating idea, you can then practice looping it around to get the entire lick.

● Look at the first four notes; this is the basic phrase we'll be repeating. For the notes on the B string, use your 1st finger on the 12th fret and 3rd finger on the 15th fret. For the bend you can either use your 2nd finger or 3rd finger. If you're new to bending then you may find using your 3rd finger the easier of the two options

● I suggest using down picks on the B string notes. Then attack the bend with an up pick

● Learn this short phrase and practice playing it. Get the timing solid, the bend under control and the notes clear and even in volume. When you can do that...

● Play the phrase 5 times to get the whole lick. Make sure neither the rhythm nor the timing crumble as you loop it. Keep it slow, accurate and in time before speeding it up

● After you've played the lick five times, play the B string at the 12th fret, then finish with the bends at the 15th fret on the B string in the final bar. These are the same bends we began the solo with: more repetition!

Lick 5

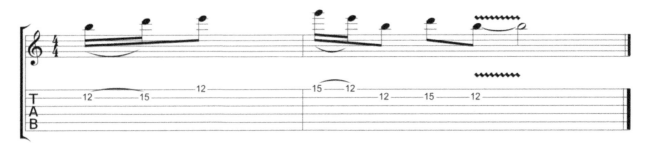

End with this simple pentatonic phrase using hammer-ons and pull-offs.

- Use your 1st and 3rd fingers to play this lick. Keep the hammer-ons and pull-offs in time and controlled. Tap your finger on firmly when hammering on and 'flick' your finger firmly off the string when pulling off to get the notes clear and sharp. Developing this control now will eventually add clarity and punch to *everything* you play, it's worth the extra effort!
- To end the solo, use your 1st finger to play and vibrato the 12th fret on the B string. 'Push' vibrato will work best here

… and that's how you play *Sweet William!* There will probably be a few things in this solo which will test you, but persevere. Mastering this solo will pay off in your quest to become a good blues player, so don't rush it! Take your time and get everything right.

Remember to check out the mini lesson and demo of *Sweet William* at **www.bluesguitarbook.com** While you're there, download the free audio demo and backing track that go with the solo.

Sweet William: Blues Power Moves

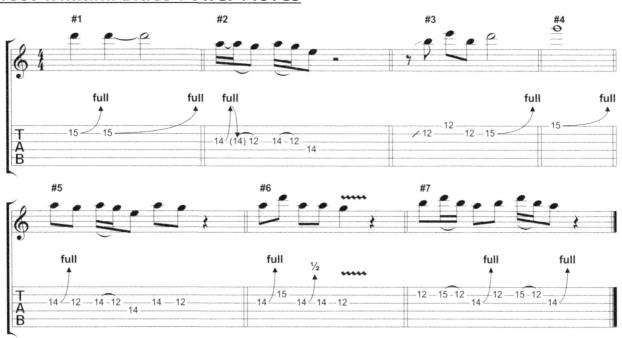

Here are some of the key components making up the licks in *Sweet William*. Remember:

- Learn each **Blues Power Move**
- Practice finding them in the shape 1 scale shape
- Make up two licks of your own based on each Power Move. Tab your licks out in your *'Guitar Practice Workbook'* (find out more about the workbook at the back of this book)
- Practice using these ideas over the *Sweet William* backing track. Compose your own solo in a similar style, or see how you can use them to improvise licks or solos of your own

Good luck with *Sweet William* and when you're ready I'll see you in the next chapter. There we'll be examining the 'sliding' blues and minor pentatonic scales and the playing of blues legend Eric Clapton.

Use the tab below to write out any ideas you discover whilst working through this chapter.

Lesson 4:
'Sliding' Scale Patterns and
Blues Brew Solo Study

In the mid 1960's a bunch of young British musicians were inspired by the sounds they heard on American blues records to create their own take on the blues. The resulting explosion in the popularity of blues has become known as the British Blues Boom. Some of the key players from this era of blues were Peter Green, Mick Taylor, Jeff Beck and perhaps the most influential of them all, Eric Clapton.

With the supergroup Cream and later on his own, Clapton went on to become a household name and an enduring and influential rock player. Later on in his career he returned to playing the blues music that inspired him originally.

In this lesson we're going to look at the **Blues Brew** solo study. This is modelled on the style of Eric Clapton and is loosely based on the track 'Strange Brew' by Cream. *Blues Brew* makes extensive use of **sliding scale patterns**. These alternative scale patterns are extremely powerful tools for the blues guitarist and it's time we took a look at them.

The 'Sliding' Minor Pentatonic Pattern

See my demonstration of the sliding scales at **www.bluesguitarbook.com**

Instead of going *across* the fingerboard as in shape 1, it is possible to *rearrange* the five notes in the minor pentatonic scale to create a pattern which goes *along* the fretboard. Just as with shape 1, this scale shape is 100% moveable: simply use the E string root note to move it into other keys.

So, you now have an alternative way to play the minor pentatonic scale. This is incredibly useful, allowing you to 'open up' the guitar neck and find all sorts of cool new sounds! Let's see this in action, here is the A minor pentatonic scale shape we saw earlier:

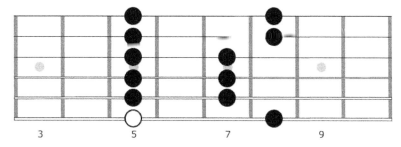

Here is the sliding A minor pentatonic pattern. Notice how it is the same until you reach the G string, when we start to move up the neck to reach some higher notes:

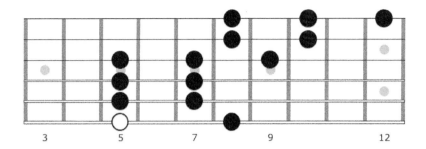

Play both scale patterns and you'll hear that they basically sound the same. They are the same! The sliding pattern still only contains 5 notes, even if it looks as if there are more. Conveniently, both patterns share the same root note too, making it easy to move them into different keys together.

With the shape 1 pattern and the sliding pattern you now have *two* different methods for playing the *same* scale. As we'll see, this gives us much more flexibility in terms of the kind of blues licks we can play.

Don't underestimate the power of these sliding scale shapes, you'll be amazed at just how many awesome blues licks are hiding inside them!

Sliding Blues Scales

Remember how we added an extra note into the pentatonic pattern to get the blues scale? Well, this note can be added into the sliding pattern too, giving us a cool *sliding blues scale* pattern. The added *b*5th note is shown as a black diamond shape in this diagram:

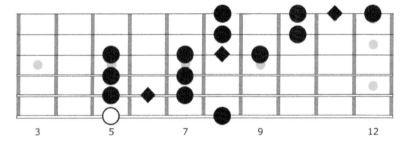

Hopefully you've worked out by now that all these patterns are the same thing and are therefore completely interchangeable. With practice you'll be zipping up and down them without even thinking about what pattern you're in!

And that's how you play the sliding minor pentatonic and blues scale shapes.

Get to know *all* of these scale patterns as well as you can. You see, the scales we've seen so far are the ones most players use the majority of the time, even the really famous ones! Learn them thoroughly and you'll have almost as much scale knowledge as some pretty legendary blues guitar players (cool huh?).

The next step is to see the sliding scales in action and to start learning a vocabulary of musical ideas that come from them. The *Blues Brew* solo up next will help with this.

Blues Solo 3: *Blues Brew*

Description:	Vintage blues solo in the style of British blues legend Eric Clapton introducing the 'sliding' blues scale
Key:	A
Will improve your:	String bending and vibrato technique, sliding blues scale knowledge and understanding of the fretboard
Watch me play it here:	**www.bluesguitarbook.com**

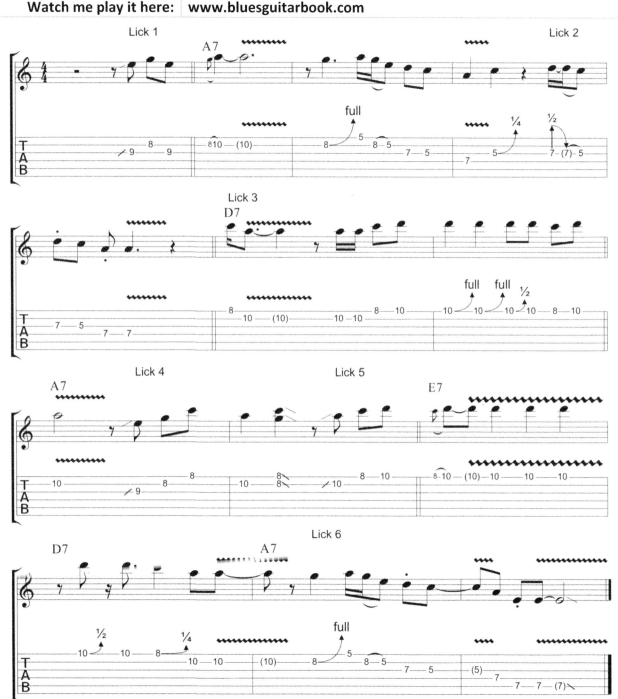

Follow the performance notes and tips as before.

Scales Used in *Blues Brew*

The licks in this solo come from shape 1 A minor pentatonic and blues scale patterns and the sliding shapes we looked at a moment ago.

Lick 1

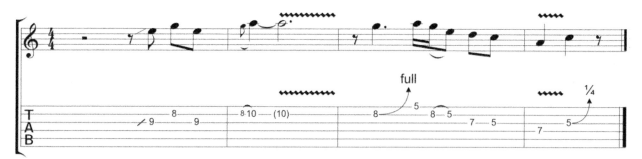

We kick off with this Clapton style blues lick featuring a couple of great sliding blues scale moves. It also shows you how the sliding and non-sliding scale patterns can be woven together.

- Use your 2nd finger to slide into the first note of the solo. This puts your 1st finger in prime position for playing the next note. It also puts your 3rd finger in position to play what's coming in the second bar
- Notice the hammer-on which starts the second bar. Play the 8th fret on the B string with your 1st finger. Pick it, then quickly hammer on to the 10th fret with your 3rd finger. You don't want to hear the 8th fret note for long, it's just a cool way of getting into the 10th fret note. These little 'decorations' are often called *grace notes*
- Check your vibrato technique as you apply vibrato to the B string at the 10th fret!
- Next, we move back down into the shape 1 minor pentatonic pattern to finish off the lick. Not much to worry about here, just get the bend solid and in tune and watch the timing is correct. Also watch the little blues curl which ends the lick in the final bar

Lick 2

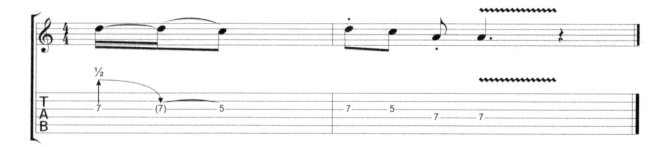

This short lick introduces a new type of bend: the *pre-bend*. This is when you bend a string up *before* you pick it. You don't hear the string being bent up, you just hear it already bent. Often after being picked you hear it being let back down again.

- Bend the G string at the 7th fret up a semi-tone or half step (1 fret in pitch). Don't pick it yet!
- Now pick the bent string, let it down and pull off to your 1st finger at the 5th fret (you just did a pre-bend!)
- If you have trouble getting the right pitch, practice the bend a few times to learn how hard you need to push the string. Then return to the pre-bend again and it should be easier

Lick 3

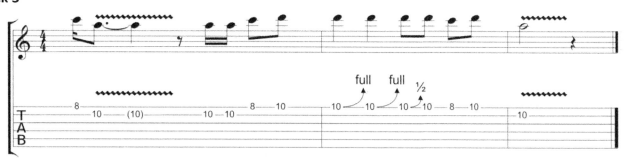

This lick shows you some of the most powerful moves from the top part of the sliding scale. You can do an insane amount of cool sounding stuff with the simple bends and ideas shown in this lick, so learn it well.

- Lots of vibrato practice in the first bar! Use your 3rd finger and remember to get the vibrato rhythmic and even (see vibrato guidelines in last chapter)
- In the second bar we've got a whole-step bend on the top E string. Listen to players like Albert King and Stevie Ray Vaughan to hear this important bend used time and time again. Use your 3rd finger to bend the note, backed up with your previous two fingers (and of course, check your bending technique is correct!)
- Look out for the sneaky little half-step bend midway through the second bar, make sure not to bend it up a whole-step by mistake

Lick 4

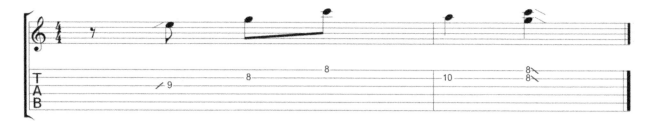

This one sounds like an 'answer' to the previous lick. Can you hear what I mean?

- By starting with your 2nd finger, you're putting your 1st finger in position to play the 8th fret notes which follow
- The lick ends with a double-stop on the top two strings at the 8th fret. A 'double-stop' is two strings played together. Play this one by flattening your 1st finger down on both strings
- After playing the double-stop, let it ring for a moment, then slide your finger down the neck towards the head of the guitar. As you do so, gradually release the pressure on the strings so that the notes eventually die out as you slide

Lick 5

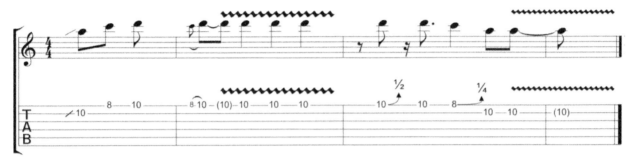

Now we're back up in the top part of the sliding minor pentatonic or blues scale shape for more vibrato and bending.

- Remember the grace note hammer-on in Lick 1? Well we're doing that again at the start of the second bar. Pick the 8th fret on the top E string and quickly hammer on your 3rd finger to the 10th fret. After hammering on, add vibrato
- For the rest of this bar we're picking the 10th fret on the top E string note as we vibrato it. Great vibrato practice, remember to follow all the vibrato 'rules'!
- Watch the tuning on the half-step bend and blues curl in the third bar. Keep checking and fine tuning your bending and blues curl technique as you go!

Lick 6

The solo finishes with a typical Clapton ending lick taken from the shape 1 minor pentatonic or blues scale.

- Make sure to get the opening bend in tune. Also remember to kill the bend off with your picking hand before you let the B string down after the bend. Get into the habit of doing this and over time your bends will start to sound super-slick
- Get the lick in time to give the solo a tidy ending. Always remember that a sloppy ending will spoil the overall effect of your performance!

... and that's how you play *Blues Brew*. Even though we've only scratched the surface, you can probably see the power of the sliding scale patterns. They help you easily access loads of killer blues soloing ideas and licks. We'll be using these a lot in the remaining solos in this book series to help you master using them.

Remember to check out my mini lesson and demo of *Blues Brew* at **www.bluesguitarbook.com**

Also download the free audio demo and backing track to practice playing *Blues Brew* along to.

Blues Brew: Blues Power Moves

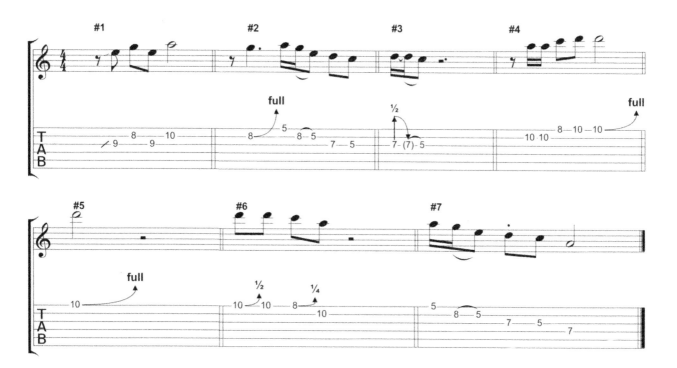

Above are some of the key components making up the licks in *Blues Brew*. Many of these are from the sliding scale patterns from this chapter.

As before:

- Learn each **Blues Power Move**
- Practice finding them in whatever scale shape they come from
- Make up two licks of your own based on each Power Move. Tab your licks out in your *'Guitar Practice Workbook'* (find out more about the workbook at the back of this book)
- Practice using these ideas over the *Blues Brew* backing track. You can use them to compose your own solo in the style of *Blues Brew* or see how you can use them to improvise licks/solos of your own

Then in no time you'll be playing your own blues licks using the ideas in this solo!

I hope you enjoy learning to play *Blues Brew* and studying the other ideas we've looked at in this chapter.

We've covered some really powerful concepts and ideas in this lesson. Explore and learn to use them as well as you can and over time they will make a *really big* difference to the sound of your blues playing.

When you're ready to move on I'll see you in the next chapter where we'll be looking at playing *Windy City*: a cool Chicago blues style solo.

Use the tab below to write out any ideas you discover whilst working through this chapter.

Lesson 5:
The 'Major 3rd Trick' and Windy City Solo Study (Chicago Blues Style!)

Welcome to Lesson 5 and well done for making it this far!

In this lesson we're going to keep adding to your blues knowledge by studying **Windy City**, a speedy Chicago blues style solo. But first, let's look at a common trick musicians have been using since the earliest days of the blues: adding the *major 3rd* into their riffs and solos.

Adding the 'Major 3rd' to the Minor Pentatonic Scale

Time for a bit of simple music theory...

As the name suggests, the minor pentatonic scale is a 'minor' type scale. This is because it contains a note we call the 'minor 3rd'. It is this note which actually *defines* a scale or a chord as being 'minor'.

Major type scales don't contain a 'minor 3rd', precisely *because* they are major and not minor! Instead, they contain a note called the 'major 3rd'. This is the note that defines a scale or chord as being 'major'.

So, the difference between major and minor chords or scales is basically the kind of 3rd they have (i.e. major or minor).

See **Chapters 5-6** on *intervals* in my **'No Bull Music Theory for Guitarists'** book for a more detailed explanation of major and minor 3rds. For now, let's carry on...

Major and minor 3rds are kind of 'opposites'. For this reason, in the traditional music rulebook, you wouldn't normally find a chord or a scale which contained them both. This is where the blues breaks the rules!

You see, even though the major 3rd doesn't belong in a minor type scale, it is sometimes added into the minor pentatonic scale. Why? Basically, when playing blues it just sounds cool! It is also one of the notes in the first chord played in the 12 bar blues, so whilst it isn't in the minor pentatonic scale, it will actually fit with the blues chord sequence. But we don't care about that, all that matters is that the result is some wicked blues licks with a hint of 'major sound' to them.

The most common place to add a major 3rd is on the G string. In the following diagram the minor 3rd is shown as **b3**. The major 3rd is one fret above it and shown as a triangle labelled **3**. We're using shape 1 G minor pentatonic scale in this example:

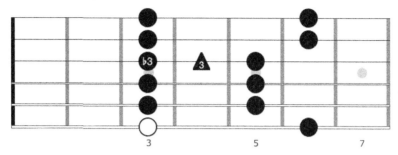

Learn the location of the major 3rd in relation to the minor pentatonic scale. You don't want to add it in all the time (sometimes it won't work at all!), just look out for it being used in any licks you learn. It is found in many classic blues licks, some of which you'll see in *Windy City*.

And That's Major 3rds….

We could go into more detail on this topic, but let's just keep it simple for now. Just remember this: the major 3rd is sometimes added into minor pentatonic and blues scale licks because it sounds cool. Nuff said...

Blues Solo 4: *Windy City*

Description:	Chicago blues solo in the style of players like Buddy Guy, Hound Dog Taylor, Magic Sam and others!
Key:	G
Will improve your:	String bending and vibrato technique, fret-hand stretch, double-stop blues licks, sliding blues scale knowledge
Watch me play it here:	**www.bluesguitarbook.com**

The 1950's was a period of mass migration in the US, as poor workers from southern US states travelled north to cities like Chicago in search of work. The result; the cross-pollination of the raw, Delta blues sound with the urban sound of electric instruments and amplification. A new style of electric blues was born, which came to be known as **Chicago Blues**. Important Chicago blues guitarists include Muddy Waters, Otis Rush, Buddy Guy, Elmore James, Magic Sam and Hound Dog Taylor.

Windy City is a Chicago blues style guitar solo. Most of the licks are straight forward, but the quicker tempo may test you a little. The solo mainly uses the G minor pentatonic scale, both shape 1 and the sliding shapes. Look out for the added *major 3rd* too!

Try to mimic the guitar sound on this one, you want lots of attack to make these licks sound authentic. The bridge pickup on your guitar with a little overdrive will probably work best.

Let's get started!

Scales Used in *Windy City*

The licks in this solo come from G minor pentatonic, both shape 1 and the sliding pattern:

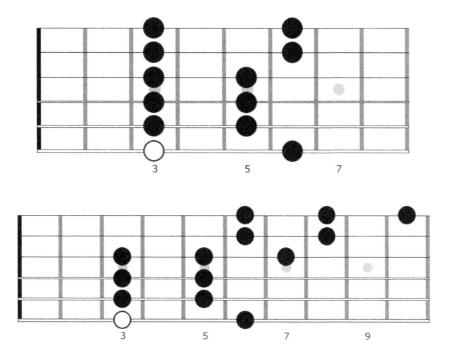

Lick 1

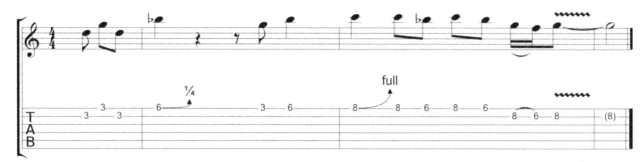

This cool lick heralds the start of the solo. Nothing too complicated here…

- We start off in G minor pentatonic shape 1. Use a 1st finger 'roll' to play the first set of notes at the 3rd fret. Then use your 3rd finger to play the 6th fret notes on the top E in the second bar. The stretch may test you a bit, but eventually the licks will be easier to play this way. Also watch the blues curls and get them sounding right
- In the third bar we move up into the top part of the sliding minor pentatonic scale. Use your 3rd finger for the 8th fret bend and remember to back it up, it will take some push to get in tune!

Lick 2

A simple picked phrase from the top part of the sliding pattern.

- Use your 2nd finger to start the lick. This puts your 1st and 3rd fingers in position and ready for the top string notes which follow
- Use your 1st finger to bend the 6th fret on the top E up slightly to get a blues curl

Lick 3

This short lick is pretty simple. It uses the top part of the sliding minor pentatonic pattern.

- Start off with your 2nd finger. This puts your other fingers in position for the rest of the lick
- Play the phrase with a fair amount of attack and watch the 1st finger vibrato at the start of the second bar
- When pulling off from the 8th to the 6th fret on the B string, pull your 3rd finger slightly downwards towards the floor as it executes the pull-off. It will 'flick' the string, making the note you are pulling off ring out more clearly

Lick 4

A cool Chicago style double-stop lick! Notice how the more 'chordal' sound of the double-stops creates a nice contrast to the other licks. One of the double-stops uses the B string at the 5th fret.

This note is not in the minor pentatonic or blues scale. We'll be looking at why this is in '**Blues Soloing for Guitar, Volume 2: Levelling Up**'.

For now, just get the lick sounding bluesy and rockin'!

- Which fingers you use for these double-stops can make the difference between them being easy or difficult! For the first double-stop at the 7th and 6th fret, use your 3rd finger on the G string and your 2nd finger on the B string. Get the double-stop sounding good before you worry about the slide into it!
- You could play the double-stop at the 5th fret a few different ways. I'd recommend you barre both strings with your 3rd finger (flatten it down to play both notes). This leaves you in a good position to...
- Play the double-stop at the 3rd fret with your 1st finger. Barre it over both notes. Now you can easily put your 2nd finger on to play the G string at the 4th fret for the final double-stop
- Did you spot the use of the major 3rd in the last double-stop? If so, then great!
- The lick finishes off with a cool little shape 1 lick. Check your vibrato technique on the final note at the end of the second bar!

Lick 5

A fairly basic G minor pentatonic lick. Play it with lots of 'snap' for that Chicago sound!

Listen to me on the video demo to hear what I mean **www.bluesguitarbook.com**

- This is a great lick for building fret hand stretch. I play the whole lick using just my 1st and 3rd fingers. Persevere with this stretch if it feels a bit tough, it will get easier (I promise...)
- Check your pull-offs and hammer-ons have a good amount of attack and get the rhythm of the phrase 100% solid. This is a rhythmic, funky lick, so make sure to get it sounding like that
- Don't miss the little grace note hammer-on at the start of the third bar

Lick 6

We wrap up the solo with this tasty ending lick making use of the added major 3rd on the G string at the 4th fret):

- Important: start the lick with your 2nd finger. Then, when you slide from the 3rd fret up to the 4th fret (from the minor 3rd to the major 3rd) your fingers will be perfectly in position to play the next run of notes
- At the end of the second bar we're using the minor 3rd to major 3rd move again. This is a really common way to use these two notes, so remember it! To play it...
- Use your 3rd finger to play the D string at the 5th fret. Play the G string at the 3rd fret with your 1st finger, then hammer your 2nd finger on to the 4th fret (that's the minor 3rd to major 3rd move, right?)

... and that's how you play *Windy City*. Hopefully this solo study has helped you build on your knowledge of the different scales we've studied, as well as given you the chance to practice and improve bending, vibrato and other essential techniques.

Remember to check out my mini lesson and video demo of *Windy City* at **www.bluesguitarbook.com**

Also download the free *Windy City* backing track and audio demonstration. Then you can practice playing the solo along with them when you're ready.

Windy City: Blues Power Moves

Here are some of the key components making up the licks in *Windy City*. Look out for that added major 3rd in some of these as you go through them.

Remember:

- Learn each **Blues Power Move**
- Practice finding them inside the scale shapes they come from
- Make up two licks of your own based on each Power Move. Tab your licks out in your *'Guitar Practice Workbook'* (find out more about the workbook at the back of this book)
- Practice using these ideas over the *Windy City* backing track. Compose your own solo in the style of *Windy City*, see how you can use them to improvise licks/solos of your own, or do both!

I hope you enjoy learning *Windy City* and exploring some of the ideas presented here. Remember, the 'exploration' that goes with learning these solos is a crucial part of building your own 'lick library' or soloing vocabulary; don't neglect to do it.

When you're ready I'll see you in the next lesson where we'll study *Don't Rush!*, a funk blues solo in the style of Freddie King and Otis Rush. We're also going to look at the theory behind the 12 bar blues a little more.

Have fun and see you in Lesson 6!

Use the tab below to write out any ideas you discover whilst working through this chapter.

Lesson 6:
More 12 Bar Blues Theory and *Don't Rush!* Solo Study (Funky Blues Style!)

Welcome to the final lesson in Volume 1 of **Blues Soloing for Guitar**!

In this lesson we're going to complete your understanding of the **12 bar blues** by going a little deeper into the theory behind it. Then we're going to study **Don't Rush!** - a fun and funky blues solo based on the playing of blues legends Freddie King and Otis Rush. Let's get started!

The 12 Bar Blues: I-IV-V Chords, Quick Change Blues and More!

This book isn't really about blues chords but the following knowledge is a 'must know' for any serious student of blues guitar. It will help you understand blues better *and* solo with more musicality and confidence. Let's get into it...

'One-Four-Five': What's It All About?

Musicians often talk about chords using numbers like *'one, four, five'*. Understanding this is really helpful in understanding why the 12 bar blues sounds the way it does.

The three chords in a 12 bar blues can be labelled with numbers. This is usually done using Roman numerals. Let's apply it to the 12 bar blues in the key of A. First let's number the chords with Roman numerals.

A7 is I (*chord 1*)
D7 is IV (*chord 4*)
E7 is V (*chord 5*)

Here they are applied to the 12 bar blues in A. Notice the chords have been labelled with I, IV or V:

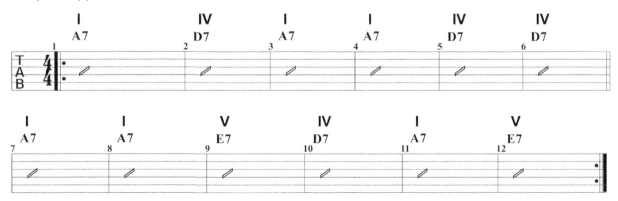

So, what does all this mean? Well, it makes it possible to describe the 12 bar blues chord sequence as a pattern of the I, IV and V chords like this:

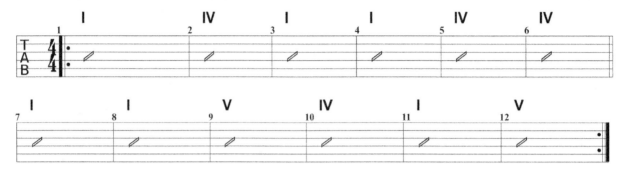

The formula could be written:

I chord for 1 bar, **IV** chord for 1 bar, **I** chord for 2 bars, **IV** chord for 2 bars, **I** chord for 2 bars, **V** chord for 1 bar, **IV** chord for 1 bar, **I** chord for 1 bar, **V** chord for 1 bar.

This pattern of the I, IV and V chords is what the 12 bar blues *really* is. It's like the 'template' you use to play a 12 bar blues.

Knowing this makes it easy to play a 12 bar blues in *any* key because the order of the I, IV and V chords always remains the same. You just need to know which chord is I, which chord is IV and which chord is V and play them at the right time.

Let's say you wanted to play a 12 bar blues in the key of G:

G7 is **I**, C7 is **IV**, D7 is **V**

All you need to do is to apply the correct pattern of the I, IV and V chords to G7, C7 and D7 and you'd get a 12 bar blues in the key of G:

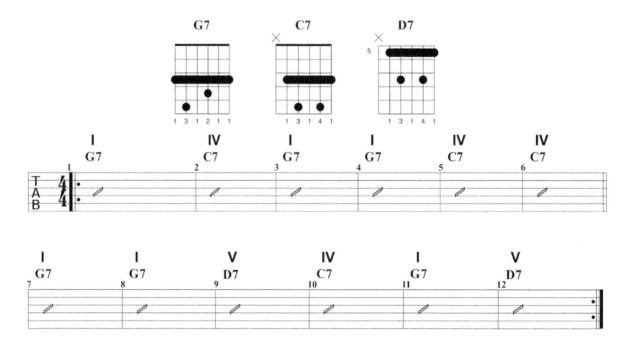

In the key of E, the I chord is E7, IV is A7 and V is B7. Put these in the right order and the result is a 12 bar blues in the key of E:

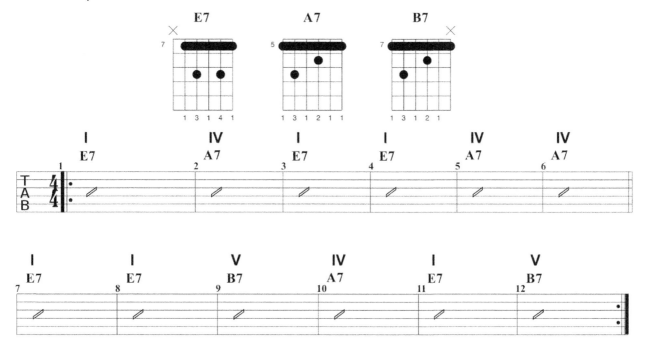

Notice how in both these examples the sequence of I, IV and V remains *exactly the same* even though the chords themselves are different.

The best way to see this theory at work is to practice playing the 12 bar blues in various keys. You'll get so used to how the sequence sounds that eventually, sticking to the 12 bar blues 'template' will become something you can just do without even thinking about it!

The 'Quick Change' Blues

The 12 bar blues format I've given you uses the IV chord in bar 2, then returns to the I chord in bar 3.

This is sometimes called a '**quick change**' blues.

Sometimes you'll see a 12 bar blues which is *not* a quick change blues. In this case you don't go to the IV chord in bar 2, instead you stay on the I chord:

We've actually seen this variation used already in *Blues Brew* and *Windy City*. Look back at the chord sequences used in those solos and you'll see the same chord is used for bars 1-4.

Blues musicians use both variations of the 12 bar blues so if you're playing with other musicians it's a case of listening and trying to hear which variation they are using, or maybe even asking. With practice and experience you'll begin to instantly recognise which version of the 12 bar blues is being used and adapt your playing to fit the rest of the band!

Here are the I, IV and V chords in some common blues keys. Using any chord shapes you know, practice playing the 12 bar blues sequence in each of these keys. You can use the *quick change* version or play the I chord only in bars 1-4. For some handy chord shapes, see Appendix 2 at the back of this book.

KEY	I	IV	V
A	A7	D7	E7
G	G7	C7	D7
D	D7	G7	A7
E	E7	A7	B7
F	F7	Bb7	C7

Should you memorise the I, IV and V chords in these keys?

This is a great idea and it's well worth the effort. You don't need to do them all now, but try and memorise this table over the next few months (it's easier than you might think!).

Now, Test Yourself!

We can number the chords in a 12 bar blues I, IV and V. Fill in the gaps in the sequence of I, IV and V below to give a 12 bar blues:

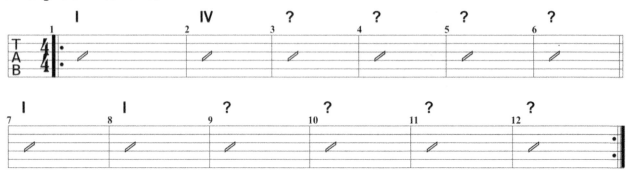

The 12 bar blues format that uses the IV chord in bar 2 is called a _____.

Check Your Answers and Let's See How You Did:

The sequence of I, IV and V in a 12 bar blues is:

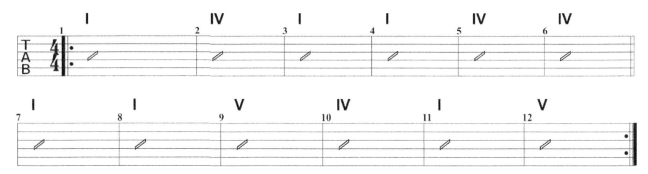

The 12 bar blues format that uses the IV chord in bar 2 is called a **quick change** blues.

Blues Solo 5: *Don't Rush!*

Description:	A funky style blues solo based on the guitar styles of Freddie King and Otis Rush
Key:	D
Will improve your:	Blues vocabulary, general speed and fluency across the guitar, string bending and vibrato technique
Watch me play it here:	**www.bluesguitarbook.com**

This solo in the key of D demonstrates just how great blues can sound when it's played with a funky rhythmic feel. Rhythmic grooves like this have been used by most blues players in some of their songs. I love how Freddie King and Otis Rush play blues in this style, which is why I've made *Don't Rush!* a sort of tribute to these two blues guitar legends.

The solo itself is pretty straight forward although the tempo might catch you out in places. The speed of some of the bends might be a challenge as well, making *Don't Rush!* a great workout for building all round fluency as a player and a great way to close out Volume 1 of this book series.

Let's break the solo down.

Scales Used in *Don't Rush!*

The licks in this solo come from D minor pentatonic up around the 10th fret. We're using shape 1 as well as the sliding patterns:

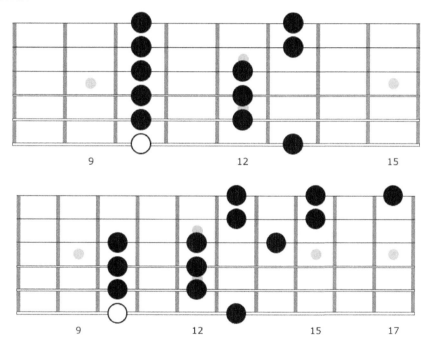

Lick 1

This cool starting lick is packed full of powerful blues moves using the top part of the sliding minor pentatonic scale. Freddie and Otis used these ideas a lot, but you'll also hear similar ideas in the playing of Albert King and Stevie Ray Vaughan. The lick is not too complicated, but the bends need to be spot-on to get it sounding really great.

- In this lick, we're repeatedly bending the 15th fret on the top E string up a tone/whole-step. I'd recommend using your 3rd finger for this (backed up by your 1st and 2nd of course!). This is a classic blues bending move, so take it and master it!
- Getting the bends clean will help you nail this lick. Bend the string quickly up to pitch and check the tuning is correct. We don't want to hear the bend being let down here either, so use your picking hand to mute the bend before you begin to let the string down. Do this for each bend in this lick

Lick 2

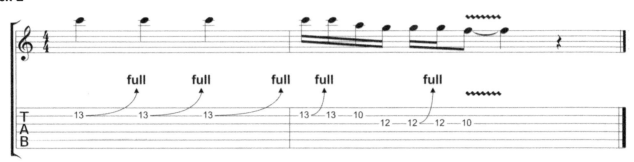

Now we move down into the shape 1 scale pattern. A fairly simple lick, but getting the timing, speed and attack right might just test you a bit.

- I'd suggest using 1st and 3rd fingers to play this lick
- Bend the B string 13th fret up using your 3rd finger. 'Kill off' each bend by muting with your pick hand, as described in Lick 1. This will give the bends definition and punch
- Watch the timing and clarity of the notes in the second bar. It's easy to rush this part, losing some of the notes. Notice how these notes are picked rather than played using hammer-ons or pull-offs. This gives them that funky attack!

Lick 3

This lick begins with a cool sliding move along the G string, taken from the sliding scale shape.

- In the first bar, use your 3rd finger for the G string slide to the 14th fret and your 2nd finger for the B string at the 13th fret. This keeps your fingers in a good position to slide back down to the 12th fret with your 3rd finger at the end of the bar and use your 1st finger to play the 10th fret note that follows
- We move back up into the sliding pattern in the next bar. Add smooth, even vibrato to the string as you pick the notes at the 15th fret

Lick 4

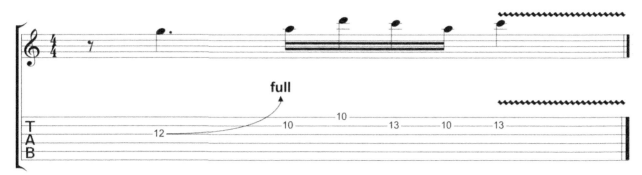

This speedy shape 1 bending lick is typical of Freddie and Otis, but also a favourite of later blues and rock players like Jimi Hendrix and Jimmy Page.

- The main challenge here is going to be the speed and timing. Slow it down so you can execute it clearly and in time, then gradually speed it up to the proper tempo
- Use your 3rd finger to play the bend and the notes at the 13th fret. The 1st finger plays all the notes at the 10th fret. Push vibrato with your 3rd finger finishes it off

Lick 5

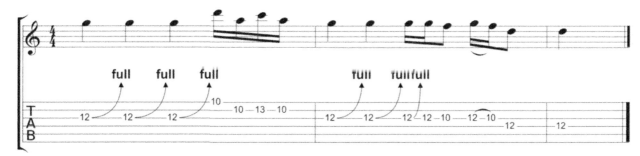

A simple but groovy sounding blues idea with repeated bends! This lick comes from shape 1 minor pentatonic.

- I'd use my 1st and 3rd fingers to play this lick
- Follow the guidelines for getting clear, controlled bends as described in the earlier licks in this solo. This helps give it a 'cutting', punchy sound which fits perfectly with the funky groove of the track
- It's easy to lose the timing with this lick, so check you're getting the rhythm correct, no notes are getting lost and that the lick has a lot of energy and 'snap' to it!

Lick 6

This shape 1 lick gives *Don't Rush!* a nice tidy ending!

- Nothing too difficult here. Just get the timing right and watch the tuning of the bends. Be careful not to bend the half-step bend midway through the first bar up too far (a common mistake!)

… and that's how you play *Don't Rush!* Remember to check out my mini lesson and demo of the whole solo at **www.bluesguitarbook.com**

Also download the free *Don't Rush!* backing track and audio demo to practice along with.

Don't Rush! Blues Power Moves

Here are some of the key components making up the licks in _Don't Rush!_

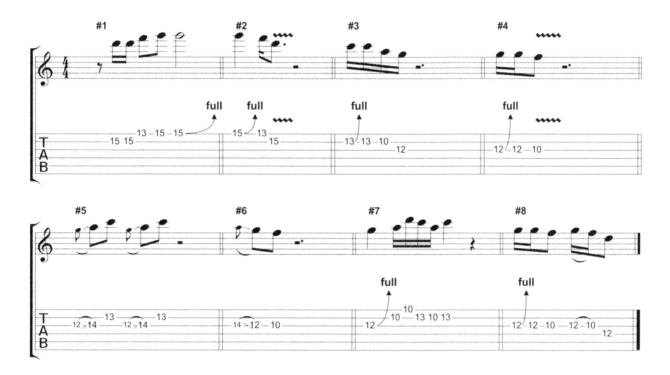

Remember:

- Learn each **Blues Power Move**
- Practice finding them in the scale shape
- Make up two licks of your own based on each Power Move. Tab your licks out in your **'Guitar Practice Workbook'** (find out more about the workbook at the back of this book)
- Practice using these ideas over the _Don't Rush!_ backing track. Compose your own solo, improvise licks/solos of your own, or ideally both, so that you absorb these moves into your blues soloing vocabulary!

That's all for now…

Enjoy _Don't Rush!_ and make sure to get it sounding funky! When you're ready, read on to discover all the good things coming in **'Blues Soloing for Guitar, Volume 2: Levelling Up'**.

Use the tab below to write out any ideas you discover whilst working through this chapter.

Final Words

You've done it - you've reached the end of *'Blues Soloing for Guitar, Volume 1: Blues Basics'*!

Congratulations! Believe it or not, you are now equipped with most of the skills and knowledge you need to become an *awesome* blues player...

But there *is* still more I need to show you, so I'm looking forward to continuing our lessons in *'Blues Soloing for Guitar Volume 2: Levelling Up'*.

In *Volume 2* you'll learn all about:

- **The Minor Blues**: another super common blues chord sequence. Discover what it is, how to play it and how to solo over it
- **Open String Soloing and Scales**: a favourite tool of blues players like Freddie King and Stevie Ray Vaughan. Learn how to use the 'twang' and power of open string soloing in *your* playing!
- **Jump Blues Style**: learn to mix up major and minor scales, chord-tones and chromatic passing notes for some cool, jazzy blues sounds!
- **High Energy Blues Repeating Licks, Double-Stops, Speedy Blues Scale Runs** and more!

It includes solo studies and licks in the styles of **BB King**, **Stevie Ray Vaughan**, **T-Bone Walker**, **Albert King** and other blues legends...

Take some time to consolidate what we've covered in this book. When you're ready I'm looking forward to finishing what we've started!

See you soon,

James

Appendix 1:
Success Tips for Learning Guitar Solos

Tip 1: Get To Know the Solo First!

Listen to the solo and get familiar with what it sounds like *before* you start learning it on the guitar. Consider learning to *sing* it: there is no better way to absorb the sounds, rhythms and feel that make it up (you don't need to be a great singer to do this!).

With this kind of preparation, you'll get the solo in your memory and under your fingers *so* much faster.

Tip 2: One Lick At A Time!

Each solo is broken up into licks. Start with the first lick and don't move on to the next until you can play it correctly and in time. It doesn't need to be as fast as it's played on the recording, just learn it thoroughly.

Once you can play two neighbouring licks, join them up. When you can play the next lick, add that on. Keep going until you can play it all.

Get the gaps between the licks *perfect!* It's *really* easy to rush into the next lick, but it's *crucial* that you get them right if you want to get the solo sounding awesome!

It takes discipline to work through a solo in this way, but it *always* pays off. You'll be playing the entire solo much better, sooner, than if you rush.

Tip 3: Get The Timing Solid!

No matter how slowly you are working through a lick, aim to get the rhythm of the lick perfect. Also get into the habit of playing everything with rhythmic energy, otherwise things can sound flat and lifeless. This is essential!

Tip 4: Practice Problem Bits The Most!

Many players mostly practice things they find easy, but to become a great player you need to devote *most* of your practice time to the things you find the hardest!

Highlight tricky licks or techniques in the tab for the solo with a highlighter pen. This makes it easy to head straight for these bits when you practice (especially if you're short on time).

Tip 5: Perfection Can Hold You Up!

Don't obsess over getting a solo perfect straight away. *Too much* attention to detail can actually hold you up! Consider getting a 'rough version' of the solo together first, *then* you can add the finishing touches, things like vibrato, blues curls etc.

Tip 6: Play Along With Me Using Video/Audio!

Once you can play a solo, put on the recording of me playing it and see if you can stay with me!

This will reveal flaws which you weren't aware of. You might be rushing a phrase, or playing something too early or late. Get your solo *totally* synched up with mine. Next play it along with the backing track on your own.

Appendix 2:
Useful Chord Shapes

The dominant 7th and dominant 9th chord shapes on the following pages work great for playing the 12 bar blues.

There are dozens of other shapes you can use too, I've just given you some of the most useful ones here - feel free to experiment with other shapes you know as well! Before you jump in, a few important points…

Root Notes

These are shown as a white disc on the diagrams.

We use the root note to move the shape around the neck to get different chords (like we did with the minor pentatonic scale shape in Lesson 1).

This is important so make sure to learn which note in the shape is the root! For more information on moving chords around using the root, see my '**No Bull Barre Chords for Guitar**' book.

Sharps and Flats

I've only given you shapes for F7, G7, A7, B7, C7, D7 and E7 but you can use these shapes to play chords like B*b*7 and C#7 too!

To get a sharp (#) chord simply move the shape up 1 fret. If you were playing F7 at the 1st fret, move it up to the 2nd fret to get F#7.

To get a flat (*b*) chord simply move the shape down 1 fret. If you were playing B7 at the 7th fret, move it down to the 6th fret to get B*b*7.

Remember there is no sharp or flat between the notes B and C or E and F. For more information on this see my '**No Bull Music Theory for Guitarists**' and '**No Bull Barre Chords for Guitar**' books.

9th Chords

Dominant 7th chords are great, but sometimes you might want a different sound. Introducing dominant 9th chords! These can 'stand in' for dominant 7th chords almost anywhere in the 12 bar blues.

Instead of playing G7, play G9. Instead of C7, play C9. It's ok to mix up 7th and 9th chords too, you don't need to stick to just one kind of chord.

Experiment with using 9th chords instead of 7th chords, they can sound really cool in blues music.

You'll find the chord shapes on the following pages, good luck!

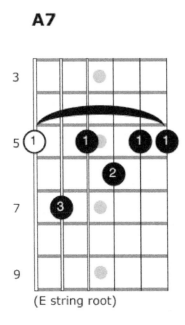

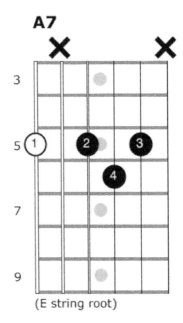

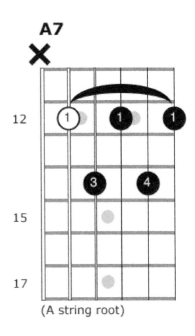

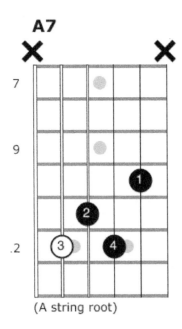

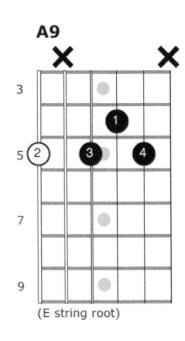

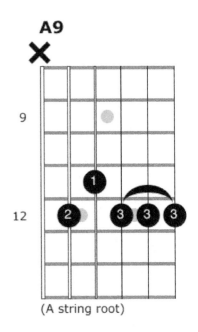

F7

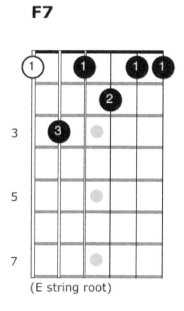

(E string root)

F7

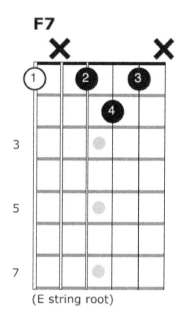

(E string root)

F7

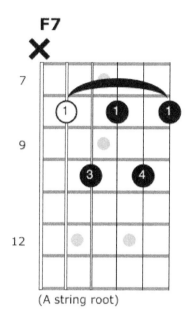

(A string root)

F7

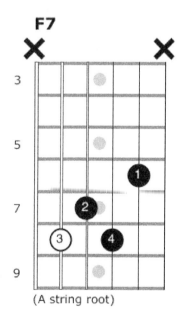

(A string root)

F9

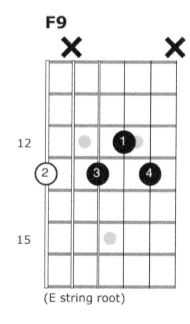

(E string root)

F9

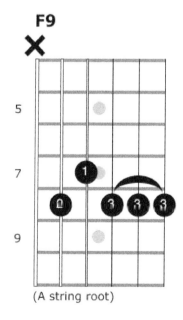

(A string root)

D7

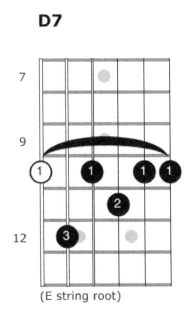

(E string root)

D7

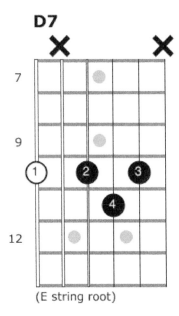

(E string root)

D7

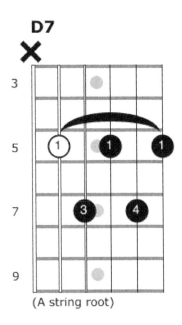

(A string root)

D7

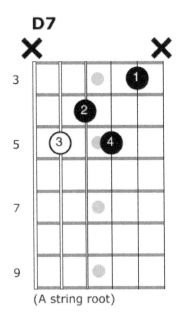

(A string root)

D9

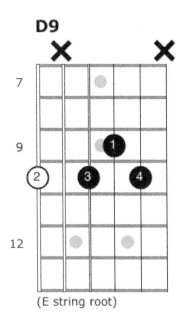

(E string root)

D9

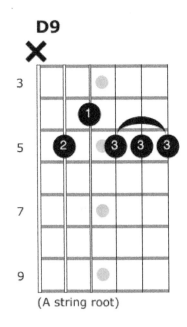

(A string root)

E7

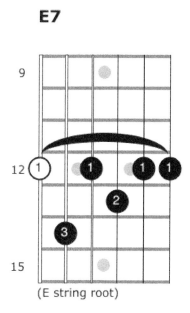

(E string root)

E7

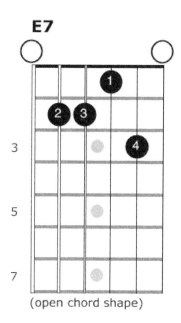

(open chord shape)

E7

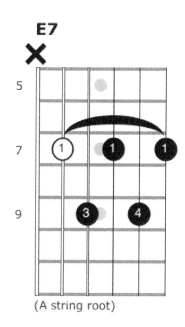

(A string root)

E7

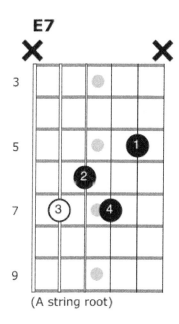

(A string root)

E9

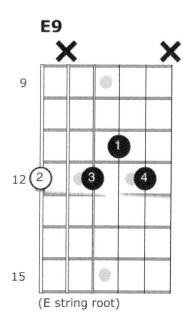

(E string root)

E9

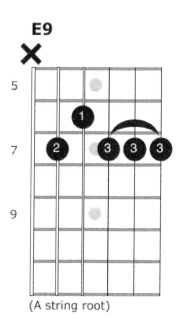

(A string root)

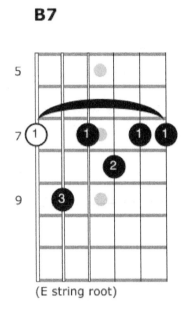

(E string root)

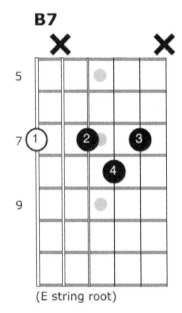

(E string root)

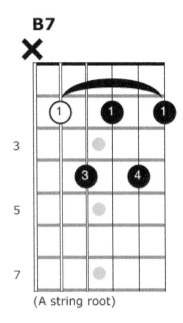

(A string root)

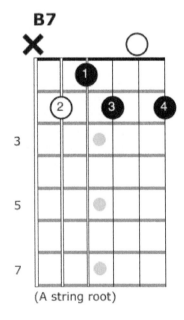

(A string root)

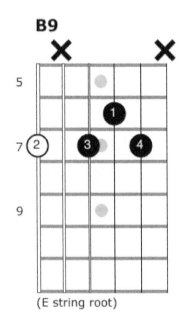

(E string root)

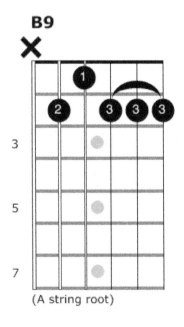

(A string root)

G7

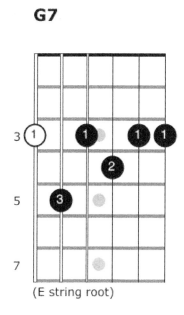

(E string root)

G7

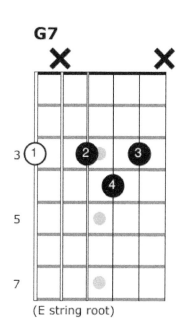

(E string root)

G7

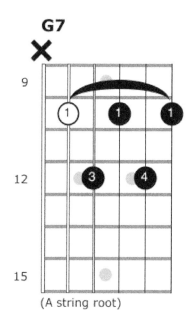

(A string root)

G7

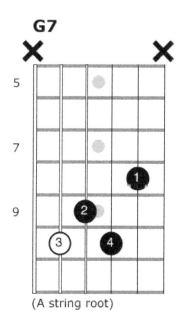

(A string root)

G9

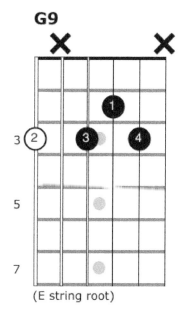

(E string root)

G9

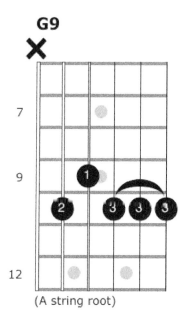

(A string root)

C7

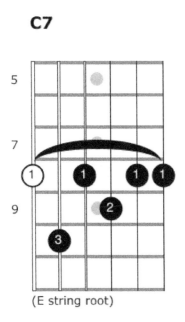

(E string root)

C7

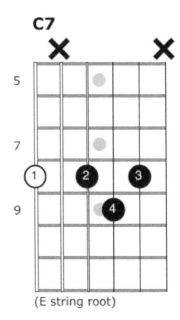

(E string root)

C7

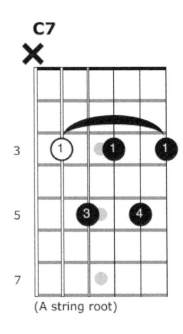

(A string root)

C7

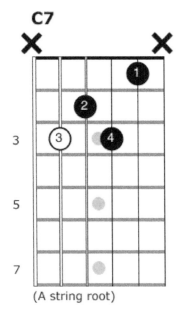

(A string root)

C9

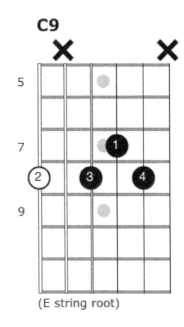

(E string root)

C9

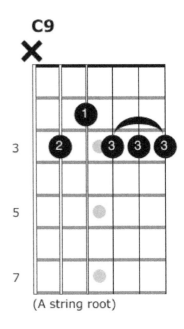

(A string root)

Further Reading

Discover other guitar books by James Shipway, all available on **Amazon**:

'Blues Soloing for Guitar, Volume 2: Levelling Up'

Blues Soloing for Guitar, Volume 2 carries on where this book leaves off. It features lessons on Minor Blues Soloing, Open String Soloing and Scales, Texas Blues Style and 'Jazzy' Blues Sounds and more.

Available on **Amazon** in Kindle and paperback with **more great video lessons and audio downloads**.

'No Bull Music Theory for Guitarists'

Master the essential music theory knowledge all guitarists need to know with *No Bull Music Theory for Guitarists*!

Understand chords, keys, intervals, scales and more and become a better musician, guitarist or songwriter. In just a few short hours, this book gives you the knowledge that most guitar players take years to accumulate... and many never truly understand. Grab your copy and get ahead of the pack!

Available on **Amazon** in Kindle and paperback with **free audiobook** included.

'No Bull Barre Chords for Guitar'

Discover a step-by-step system for mastering the essential barre chord shapes that *all* guitarists and singer-songwriter guitar players need to know!

You'll learn the most important and useful barre chord shapes and how to use them to play literally *hundreds* of possible chord sequences and songs. *Plus,* you'll discover powerful practice methods, exercises and 'memory hacks' to help you master barre chords without the headaches most players face!

Available on **Amazon** in Kindle and paperback with **free downloadable play-along practice tracks** included.

'The Guitar Practice Workbook'

The ultimate multi-purpose practice workbook for guitarists of all levels!

Featuring powerful practice hacks, important scales and chord shapes as well as over 50 pages of blank tab, fretboard diagrams and chord boxes for recording your own killer licks, exercises and song ideas.

Available on **Amazon** as a paperback with a **free downloadable 'Goal Worksheet'** to help you track your progress and reach your guitar goals!

'Blank Guitar Tab'

For guitar students, teachers, songwriters and musicians wanting to log daily practice exercises or set down new song ideas, I've put together some blank tab books, each one containing 12 blank guitar tab staves and 8 blank chord boxes for each double page spread.

The books are available on **Amazon** with 150, 100 or 65 pages.

Check Out My Total Guitar Lab Online School!

Want to study specific guitar styles and topics with me, James Shipway, as your guitar teacher? Well you can, with my online guitar community at **Total Guitar Lab!**

Join and get instant access to all my premium guitar courses plus live training, workshops and Q&A sessions. Lean more and discover the amazing results guitarists have been getting with my training at:

https://www.totalguitarlab.com

Join Me On Your Favourite Social Media Platform

Pinterest: www.pinterest.co.uk/JamesShipwayGtr/
Facebook: www.facebook.com/jamesshipwayguitar/
YouTube: Search for James Shipway on YouTube and subscribe for hours of free video lessons!

Printed in Great Britain
by Amazon